FIREFIGHTER HEROES

CITY FIREFIGHTERS

By Spencer Brinker

Consultant: Beth Gambro
Reading Specialist, Yorkville, Illinois

BEARPORT
PUBLISHING

Minneapolis, Minnesota

Teaching Tips

Before Reading

- Look at the cover of the book. Discuss the picture and the title.
- Ask readers to brainstorm a list of what they already know about firefighters. What can they expect to see in the book?
- Go on a picture walk, looking through the pictures to discuss vocabulary and make predictions about the text.

During Reading

- Read for purpose. Encourage readers to think about what city firefighters do as they are reading.
- Ask readers to look for the details of the book. What are they learning about how city firefighters put out fires?
- If readers encounter an unknown word, ask them to look at the sounds in the word. Then, ask them to look at the rest of the page. Are there any clues to help them understand?

After Reading

- Encourage readers to pick a buddy and reread the book together.
- Ask readers to name two things city firefighters do during a fire. Find the pages that tell about these things.
- Ask readers to write or draw something they learned about city firefighters.

Credits

Cover and title page, © hallojulie/iStock and © suravikin/iStock; 3, © standret/iStock; 5, © Sergey Toronto/Adobe Stock; 7, © xavierarnau/iStock; 9, © Matthew Perkins/iStock; 10, © HABY/iStock; 11, © shaunl/iStock; 13, © ollo/iStock; 14, © AU USANakul+/Adobe Stock; 15, © gorodenkoff/iStock; 16–17, © Denis Torkhov/iStock; 18, © Wavebreakmedia/iStock; 19, © Mert G/Shutterstock; 21, © wavebreak3/Adobe Stock; 22, © jondpatton/iStock and © Imagesbybarbara/iStock; 23TL, © jaroon/iStock; 23TM, © martin-dm/iStock; 23TR, © scbarney/iStock; 23BL, © fotosav/iStock; 23BM, ©poco_bw/iStock; 23BR, © Aleksey Matrenin/iStock.

See BearportPublishing.com for our statement on Generative AI Usage.

Library of Congress Cataloging-in-Publication Data

Names: Brinker, Spencer, author.
Title: City firefighters / by Spencer Brinker.
Description: Minneapolis, Minnesota : Bearport Publishing Company, [2025] |
   Series: Firefighter heroes | Includes bibliographical references and
   index.
Identifiers: LCCN 2024022423 (print) | LCCN 2024022424 (ebook) | ISBN
   9798892327176 (library binding) | ISBN 9798892327671 (paperback) | ISBN
   9798892328043 (ebook)
Subjects: LCSH: Fire extinction--Juvenile literature. | Fire
   fighters--Juvenile literature.
Classification: LCC TH9148 .B756 2025 (print) | LCC TH9148 (ebook) | DDC
   363.37092--dc23/eng/20240603
LC record available at https://lccn.loc.gov/2024022423
LC ebook record available at https://lccn.loc.gov/2024022424

For more information, write to Bearport Publishing, 5357 Penn Avenue South, Minneapolis, MN 55419.

Contents

Orange Flames

Look at that building!

Fire is coming out the windows.

The orange blaze is moving fast.

We need city firefighters!

4

5

The firefighter heroes put on special coats and hats.

Gloves cover their hands.

They wear helmets, too.

This gear keeps them safe.

Then, the heroes jump into their fire truck.

They turn on the lights and **siren**.

Wheee-whooo!

The truck speeds to the building.

The heroes get to work.

They put a big **hose** on a **hydrant**.

The hose sprays lots of water.

This stops the fire from **spreading**.

A hydrant

Hose

It looks like someone is inside the building.

The heroes climb up a ladder to get in.

They breathe from **air tanks** full of clean air.

Air tank

The firefighters find someone.

They use an axe to chop down the door.

Then, the heroes bring the person to safety.

15

The heroes spray more water.

Soon, they cannot see any fire.

The firefighters look everywhere to make sure it is out.

Firefighters in the city can help in other ways, too.

They teach people about fire safety.

Sometimes, the heroes even save animals!

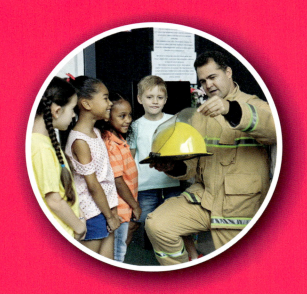

These heroes work hard every day.

They keep our city safe.

Thanks, firefighters!

A Fire Truck and Its Tools

City firefighters use a truck with special tools to stop fires.

A ladder helps firefighters reach tall places.

Flashing lights tell people the truck is going to a fire.

Fire trucks have lights to help firefighters see at night.

A loud siren tells cars to move out of the way.

Glossary

air tanks things that hold clean air

gloves coverings to keep hands safe

hose a long tube that carries water

hydrant a large outdoor pipe where hoses can get water

siren something that makes a loud sound

spreading moving to a new place

Index

Read More

Leed, Percy. *Firefighters: A First Look (Read about Community Helpers).* Minneapolis: Lerner Publications, 2025.

Rathburn, Betsy. *Firefighters (Community Workers).* Minneapolis: Bellwether Media, Inc., 2025.

Learn More Online

1. Go to **FactSurfer.com** or scan the QR code below.
2. Enter "**City Firefighters**" into the search box.
3. Click on the cover of this book to see a list of websites.

About the Author

Spencer Brinker lives in Minnesota with his family, dog, and lizard.